Personal Development

TABLE OF CONTENTS

Cover Art by
Matthew Archambault

Black & White Illustrations by
Ken Landgraf

EDCON
Publishing Group

Copyright © 2006
AV Concepts Corporation
Edcon Publishing Group

Printed in U.S.A.
ISBN# 1-55576-384-7

EDCON PUBLISHING

LEARNING HOW TO TAKE A TEST

LEARNING HOW TO TAKE A TEST

Mr. Morris begins: "I know this class likes to hear the latest news – the hottest tip. Well, today is your lucky day. I'm going to give you some tips on how to take a test.

When taking a test – any test – there are three basic conditions you must have:

> **POSITIVE MENTAL ATTITUDE**
> **ACCEPT RESPONSIBILITY FOR ACTIONS**
> **DON'T FEAR TESTS**

You must have a positive attitude toward the test, be prepared to assume responsibility for the results, and not be afraid of failure."

"My folks sure would agree with that!" said Mary. "They're always saying that a positive attitude will help you find success in life. I guess that means taking a test too. They say you must build self-confidence and have faith in yourself. Believe you will succeed, and you will. Hmmm, come to think of it, that sure didn't work for me in yesterday's hundred yard dash.

"I do assume responsibility for all my actions. And that certainly would include taking a test. If I pass, I take credit. If I fail, I can only blame myself. I'm my own boss and that's the way I like it.

LEARNING HOW TO TAKE A TEST

"I don't have any trouble with those first two – having a positive attitude and assuming responsibility – that's really part of growing up. But I'm not sure I understand the last one – fear of failure. I'm never afraid of taking a test. But, then again, I'm not overjoyed about it either. Mr. Morris, would you explain what you mean by fear of failure?"

"Sure, Mary. Let's look at the test you took last week. You knew you had to get a high grade on this test to remain on the honor roll. Think how you felt before taking the test. Were you nervous or calm?"

"I guess I was a little nervous."

"Yes," smiled Mr. Morris. "I expect you were. But you weren't overly tense or physically ill. You were concerned, but possessed no real fear of the test.
"Some students let tests upset them so much that they develop a deep-seated fear of failure – or what psychologists like to call 'test anxiety.' They become so anxious – so afraid of taking the test – that they become physically ill. They let their emotions get in the way of their performance. If we learn to become aware of our emotions, assume responsibility for our actions, and develop a positive attitude toward taking a test, then we're on the road to school success!

"Building confidence begins with quiet, independent study.

"Much of our studying can be completed during school. However, no one can MAKE you study. You must assume this responsibility and make wise use of school time. If you don't, you're only fooling yourself."

EDCON PUBLISHING

"Many times, other activities seem to be more fun," said Mary.

"Studying is hard work and you must take large doses of self-discipline," replied Mr. Morris. "Often, you have to force yourself to begin studying.

"Now for the next step. There are teacher-made tests and commercially produced tests – often called standardized tests. On the teacher-made test, you will respond to subject matter that you are presently studying. The standardized test is usually broader and will compare your results with those of a larger sample. Both of these types of tests have their purposes, advantages, and disadvantages.

SUBJECTIVE
OBJECTIVE

"Another way of classifying tests are "subjective" and "objective." The objective test relies on factual information and is easier to be scored. The objective test usually has the following types of questions:

LEARNING HOW TO TAKE A TEST

TRUE-FALSE
COMPLETION
MULTIPLE CHOICE
MATCHING
RANK IN CORRECT ORDER

"You'll take more objective tests during your school career. These require you to study for factual information – names, dates, important events.

"Subjective tests will either be short answer or essay, and they will require you to know the factual information and to be able to write it using proper grammar and spelling in a clear, readable, narrative form.

"The subjective test is considered more difficult, but many teachers believe it's a better test of your knowledge about a subject. Be sure to read the questions carefully in an essay test and pay close attention to such words as:

COMPARE
CONTRAST
DESCRIBE
LIST

"Now that you have a positive attitude for taking a test, assume responsibility for the results, have your emotions under control, and are aware of the types of tests, let's move on to some "hot tips" known by all good test takers.

"The first tip is, STUDY, STUDY, STUDY! Let's face it, studying isn't easy for most of us. But it has to be done. Learning is slow, hard work. And we must discipline ourselves in order to get it done. A great deal of studying can be done in school, but YOU HAVE TO USE YOUR TIME WISELY. Studying requires you to read, take notes, re-read, and then read again.

EDCON PUBLISHING

"Before every test, GET PLENTY OF REST and EAT A BALANCED MEAL. A rested body and a satisfied stomach are required before the mind can be fully engaged.

"Try to get to the testing site A LITTLE AHEAD OF TIME. Then sit down. Take a few deep breaths. Just relax. Close your eyes and make certain your feelings and emotions are under control.

"Make certain you BRING EXTRA PAPER AND PENCILS AND OTHER NECESSARY SUPPLIES.

"When the test administrator talks – you listen! BE ALERT. Understand every word. If you don't, ask for clarification. Don't just sit there like a bump on a log.

"FAMILIARIZE YOURSELF WITH THE FORMAT OF THE QUESTIONS AND ANSWERS. If there's a test booklet and separate answer sheet, then make certain you keep the two lined up. Re-check this alignment several times during the test.

"READ EACH QUESTION CAREFULLY. Answer the easier questions first, leaving the ones you don't know until later. You might pick up a cue from another question that will help you remember a difficult answer.

LEARNING HOW TO TAKE A TEST

"If the test requires you to read a paragraph, DON'T GET TOO INVOLVED IN THE STORY. Read only to answer the questions – and not for pleasure.

"If the test requires an essay-type answer, READ THE QUESTION SEVERAL TIMES. Take several seconds to *think* about the question – and your answer.

"ORGANIZE YOUR ANSWER. Make a few brief notes – a word outline before you begin to write. Then write your answer. Be careful with your grammar and spelling. Write clearly, and large enough to read. ALWAYS TRY TO ANSWER EVERY ESSAY QUESTION. You'll get a zero for one not answered, but even a wild guess might get you five to ten points.

"CONCENTRATE ON THE TEST. Don't let your mind wander. Don't let other students distract you – no matter how "cute" they might be. This could result in the loss of your test paper and a zero for the test.

"Tests are designed to find out what you've learned and what your teacher has taught. Tests aren't meant to punish you. They won't hurt you. Don't let yourself sink to the level of a cheater. You'll only hurt yourself in the long run.

EDCON PUBLISHING

Personal Development

"WORK QUICKLY, BUT DON'T RUSH YOURSELF.

"Time is important – be aware of it. And if there's no clock in the room, make sure you bring a watch. But remember to let time work *for* you and not *against* you.

"WORK QUICKLY, BUT BE ACCURATE. Make sure you are marking the right answer on the answer sheet. And be sure to make your marks dark! If you change an answer, make certain you erase all the old marks. Do all your figuring on scrap paper.

"When you've completed a section and the directions tell you to stop, then stop! USE THIS TIME TO REVIEW YOUR ANSWERS."

"Mr. Morris, would you help me?"
"Sure, Judy. What's the problem?"
"I just don't understand these directions."

"DON'T BE AFRAID TO ASK YOUR TEST ADMINISTRATOR FOR HELP if you don't understand something. When you have completed the test and have a little time left, don't talk to your neighbor. Use this time to review your answers, your spelling, and the answers you erased to make sure all of the marks are gone."

* * *

LEARNING HOW TO TAKE A TEST

Now, let's review some of the basic test-taking tips Mr. Morris has covered.

1. You must have a positive mental attitude toward test taking.
2. You must be able to accept responsibility for your actions.
3. You should have no fear of taking a test.
4. You must STUDY, STUDY, STUDY!
5. Get plenty of rest and eat a well-balanced meal before your test.
6. Take along extra paper and pencils.
7. Report to the room early – and relax!
8. Clean your desktop of all material.
9. Listen carefully to instructions.
10. Read directions and answer all samples.
11. Understand the testing format.
12. Think before answering.
13. Concentrate on the test.
14. Be accurate and write neatly.
15. Use correct grammar and spelling.
16. If you're not penalized, guess!
17. Be aware of the time. Work quickly, but don't rush.
18. Review! Review! Review! Use all available time.
19. After a final review of your paper, double check your answers and hand in the paper.

And feel confident that by following these simple test-taking tips, you passed another test!

EDCON PUBLISHING

Personal Development

SENTENCE COMPLETION

Use the words in the box to complete the sentences below.

desk tops	responsibility
afraid	study
meal	early and ready
mental attitude	directions
grammar	concentrate
guess	rush
questions	format
listen	eyes

1. The best way to get a good grade on a test is to

   _____.

2. You must also have a positive _____ toward test taking.

3. You must be able to accept _____ for your actions.

4. You cannot be _____ of taking a test.

5. Before every test, you must eat a well-balanced

   _____.

6. Always report to the testing room _____.

7. Clean your _____ of all books, papers, and pencils.

LEARNING HOW TO TAKE A TEST

SENTENCE COMPLETION

Use the words in the box to complete the sentences below.

desk tops	**responsibility**
afraid	**study**
meal	**early and ready**
mental attitude	**directions**
grammar	**concentrate**
guess	**rush**
questions	**format**
listen	**eyes**

8. _____ carefully to instructions.

9. Read _____ and answer all _____.

10. Try to understand the testing _____.

11. Make sure to keep your _____ on your own paper.

12. _____ on the test. Eliminate all outside thoughts.

13. Be accurate. Write neatly and use correct

    _____.

14. If not penalized, _____.

15. Work quickly, but do not _____. Review your paper when you are finished.

Answers can be found on page 45.

EDCON PUBLISHING

TEST WISENESS

TEST WISENESS

Today's fast-paced society requires each of us to be able to make knowledgeable decisions — decisions that are based on the best available data that will help us protect our environment and, at the same time, help us build a better society.

Within our society schools have been assigned the responsibility of education. In order to measure student achievement and progress, states and local schools have developed testing programs. Test results are used by teachers and principals to evaluate student learning. Each score is carefully examined in order to determine just how much each student has learned and progressed in each subject.

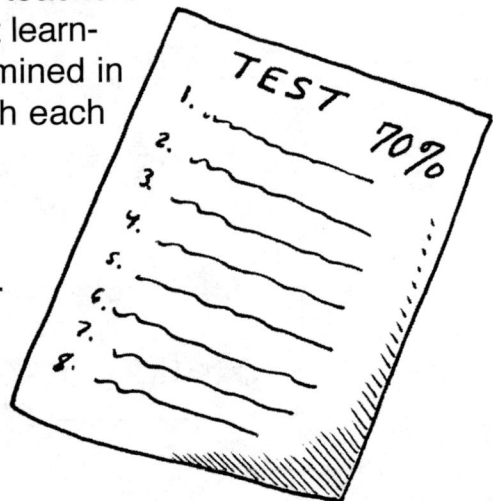

But test scores often mislead us. Some students seem to know their subject matter but, for some reason, never score high on tests.

TEST WISENESS

DRIVER EXAMINATION
PARKING
MOTORCYCLES - FIRST 4 SPACES
OPPOSITE STOP SIGN →
OTHERS - LEFT SIDE FACING
← FENCE

Let's read about Kim and her experience taking the driving exam.

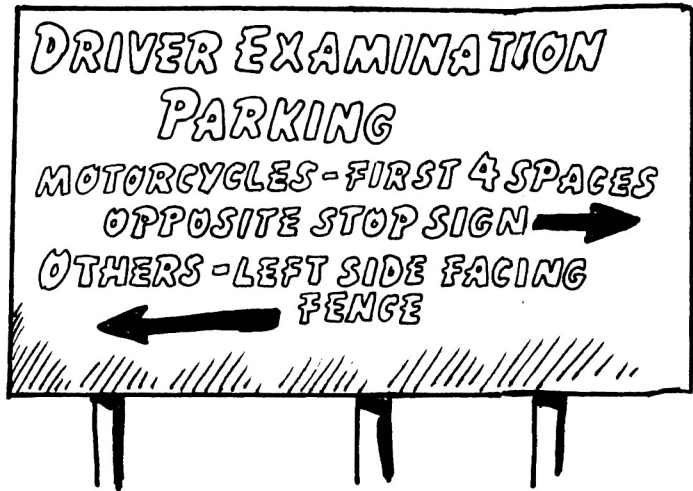

"Mr. Schaeffer, my driver education teacher, encouraged me to take the state drivers' exam. He said it would be a breeze for me.

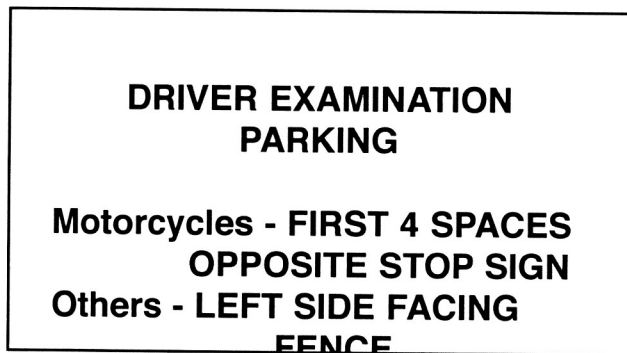

DRIVER EXAMINATION
PARKING

Motorcycles - FIRST 4 SPACES
OPPOSITE STOP SIGN
Others - LEFT SIDE FACING
FENCE

18

"It looked more like a hurricane was coming when I arrived at the testing center – real dark and overcast. But my spirits were high, and I had reviewed the manual at least 50 times. How could I fail? But when the officer began to ask me questions, I knew I was in trouble. My mind seemed to stop. I felt silly and angry at the same time. I knew the answers, but I just couldn't think at that moment."

Kim is like a lot of students. They know the subject matter much better than they are able to demonstrate.

Learning is only the first step to scoring higher on exams.

The ability to demonstrate that learning to self and others is the second and important step in scoring higher on tests.

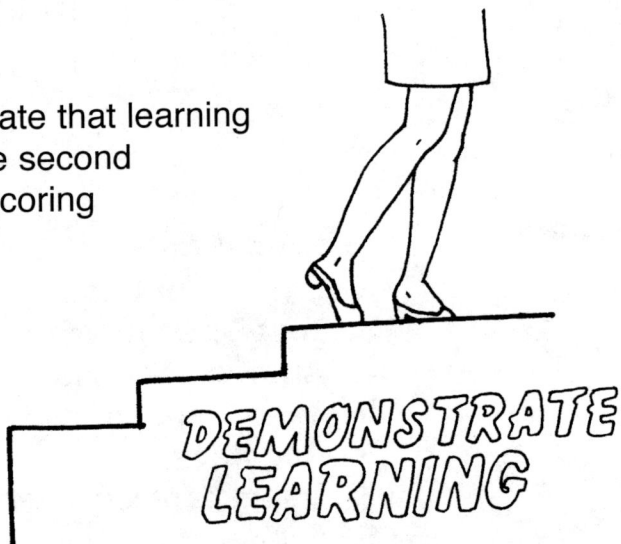

TEST WISENESS

Testwiseness is a word that has been created to describe the area of test-taking knowledges. It is independent of the subject matter on any given test.

Research has demonstrated that students who are test wise score higher on tests. Test wise students have learned to think clearly, use the characteristics of the test to their advantage, and when all else fails, follow a set of pre-established rules or guidelines.

Some students learn Testwiseness indirectly, however, most students must learn it for themselves. Logical reasoning and problem-solving skills are a real help.

Let's read as Mr. Labow reviews Testwiseness.

"Now, class, I've placed the 8 major areas of Testwiseness on the board. You must master each area if you are to become better test-takers. The 8 areas are:

1. **Mental Attitude**
2. **Emotional Conditioning**
3. **Test Directions**
4. **Answer Formats**
5. **Time Management**
6. **Accuracy**
7. **Using Test Content**
8. **Guessing**

EDCON PUBLISHING

Personal Development

"Good test takers are motivated and ready to go. They think good, positive thoughts about taking the test, and can't wait to begin.

"Good test takers are self-motivated. Some give themselves a "pep talk" like the coach does before a game. Others will use self-sentences like,

I'M GONNA SMASH MRS. HOBBS' TEST.
I'VE STUDIED, AND I'M READY.
LOOK OUT "A" HERE I COME.

"Your emotional condition can be influenced by your mental attitude. Be certain that YOU are in control. Everybody gets a little nervous before a test, so expect it. Remember the three C's – be

> **CALM**
> **COOL**
> **COLLECTED**

"There are two types of people in the world. The strong ego TYPE A person who glances at the directions, accepts the challenge, and begins the adventure of the task. The task could be taking a test, or assembling a new toy.
"The TYPE B person very carefully and slowly studies the directions before beginning the task. He doesn't turn the page or open the package before he has the directions completely read and understood.
"To become test wise, you must become a TYPE B person.

"You must read and understand all the directions before you begin each section of the test.

"Make sure you understand the vocabulary and know exactly what is expected of you. Don't be afraid to ask the test administrator if you don't understand.

TEST WISENESS

"Read the directions and make sure you understand the answer format. If you use a separate answer booklet, make sure that you're marking your answers in the correct column.

"Be certain that you have the proper marking instrument, such as a #2 pencil.

"The management of our time is one of the most important things we can learn. Being aware of the available time, and using it wisely, will improve your score.

"Take your own watch with you, and get in the habit of using it for all tests. You won't have to search for a clock, you'll feel more comfortable, it will save time, and you'll be more organized.

"Some test administrators will re-set the clock in the room when they begin to time the test. Don't let this confuse you.

EDCON PUBLISHING

TEST WISENESS

"Students who participate in sports programs have to be experts in time management. They must pace themselves. Knowing the rules of the game is easy. Being able to coordinate your physical and mental knowledge within a fixed period of time is the secret to success.

"Concentration plays a big part in being accurate – screening out all thoughts and focusing on the main task.

"Using clues, thinking about patterns, and aiming for your goal are all involved with becoming test wise."

"Mr. Labow, sometimes I read a question and I think I know the answer, but I'm not quite sure."

TEST WISENESS

"When that happens, Betty, put a small mark by the question and go on to the next question. Answer all questions that you're sure of, and then return to those you have marked. That way, you won't waste time on questions to which you don't know the answers. Also, one of the other questions might remind you of the right answer.

"Some test-wise students will read the answers BEFORE they read the paragraphs containing the question. This gives them an idea of the type of information they need to remember. Remember, this works for some, and not for others.

"If it's an essay or subjective test, then you must schedule enough time to answer all the questions. Try and answer every question on an essay test – even if you have to dream up an answer. Don't leave any blanks!

"First, read all the essay questions and select the one you know the most about to answer first – even if this is the last question. This will often get your mind in gear for the other questions.

"It's important on an essay test and/or section that you don't spend all your time on one question just because you remember a lot about it.

"All of us use our time differently, but a general rule for answering a single question on an essay test is to divide your time according to the following schedule:

1. 1/4	Outlining the Answer
2. 1/2	Writing the Answer
3. 1/4	Reviewing the Answer

"Using test content is the hardest thing for us to learn. If we aren't careful, we can "out-trick" ourselves.

EDCON PUBLISHING

"Some of these ideas should only be used as a last resort to help us with our guessing strategy. If there is no penalty for guessing – then guess! If the question has four possible answers and you can eliminate two of them, or if it's a True or False question, then you have a 50-50 chance of getting the right answer.

> The capital of Pennsylvania is
> a. Philadelphia
> b. Harrisburg
> ✗ Pittsburgh
> d. King of Prussia

"Most test-wise students will read the question and each option very carefully. They'll eliminate those options they know are not correct. In other words, they look for the wrong answers first!"

"Mr. Labow, sometimes I can find the correct answer because it's longer than the others and explains the answer more completely."

"Yes, Jim, that can give you a clue. Also, make sure the answer is grammatically correct with the stem.

"The test-wise student will recognize and make use of specific determiners such as,

Always
Never
Only
Must

"Also, he"ll use the content from one question to help him answer another.

"Now, let's quickly review the eight areas of Testwiseness before the bell rings.

MENTAL ATTITIDE

"Mental Attitude – to develop a positive attitude toward the test.

EMOTIONAL CONDITIONING

"Emotional Conditioning – to be in complete control of your feelings and emotions to maintain a cool, calm, relaxed state.

TIME MANAGEMENT

"Time Management – to learn to budget all available time to improve your performance.

DIRECTIONS

"Directions – to understand what to do, and how to do it; to know what is expected of the test taker.

ANSWER FORMAT

"Answer Format – to know where and how to answer the questions.

EDCON PUBLISHING

TEST WISENESS

ACCURACY

"Accuracy – to concentrate on the tasks and to eliminate mistakes.

USING TEST CONTENT

"Using Test Content – to learn how content can assist the test taker in selecting the correct answers.

GUESSING STRATEGY

"Guessing Strategy – to understand when to guess and how to develop a guessing plan.

"If you study and practice these 8 areas, then all of you can improve your test scores. You'll become smarter overnight – amazing your parents and shocking your teachers!

"Now, good luck as you practice your skills of Testwiseness."

TEST WISENESS

SENTENCE COMPLETION

Match each word(s) from the box to its matching statement below.

A. Using test content	F. Answer format
B. Time management	G. Emotional conditioning
C. Mental attitude	H. Accuracy
D. Testwiseness	I. Studying
E. Directions	J. Guessing Strategy

_____1. Thinking logically about the testing situation and the test itself.

_____2. To be in complete control of all your emotions and feelings. To remain in a cool, calm, relaxed state.

_____3. To develop a positive attitude toward the test.

_____4. To budget all available time to improve performance.

_____5. To know where and how to answer all the questions.

_____6. To understand what to do and how to do it. To know what is expected of the test taker.

_____7. To concentrate on the task and to eliminate mistakes.

_____8. To learn how the content can assist the test taker in selecting the correct answer.

_____9. To understand when to guess and to develop a plan for guessing.

_____10. The best way to learn and get good grades on tests.

Answers can be found on page 45.

EDCON PUBLISHING

STUDYING
AND
RETENTION

STUDYING AND RETENTION

"May I have your attention, please! I have a special announcement. Mr. Avery would like to announce that he will offer the following reward for the student achieving the highest grade on the mid-term exam: Mr. Avery will drive the winner and the winner's date to the annual Roller Dance in his antique car. He will also chauffeur them for the entire day. Further details are available from Mr. Avery."

"Wow!
I could really go for that," said Marsha. "Home, James...uh, Mr. Avery. I wonder what I would have to call him."

"Yeah," answered Pete. 'Wouldn't Laura be surprised if I picked her up in an antique car – with old Mr. Avery driving. That would be terrific!"

*　　*　　*　　*　　*

Mr. Avery seems to have supplied an important factor for learning – motivation! The ride in an antique automobile that is chauffeured by a teacher is concrete and meaningful. Motivation is needed no matter what we do. But EXTERNAL motivation and reward must be achievable in order for us to become self-motivated.

STUDYING AND RETENTION

Learning is not always easy. Students must have self-motivation in order to learn. Desire is what your teacher would call it. Wanting to learn, and having the ability to stick to the task, is a definite must. To improve one's mind or to go to college are good long-term goals. But they may be too abstract or far in the future for some students.
A more immediate tangible goal should be set – one that is difficult, but obtainable. One that has meaning for every student. And, of course, our attitude affects everything we do. We must have a positive belief in US – and our ability to study and learn. We must teach that little voice inside us to say, YOU CAN DO IT! IF OLD, WHAT'S-HER-NAME CAN GET GOOD GRADES, I SURE CAN!

Pete would like to win Mr. Avery's contest, but in order to win, he knows that he must improve his test scores. Let's listen as he talks to his friend Jeff.

"Jeff, I'd like to win Mr. Avery's contest, but I need a game plan to raise my test scores."

"I'm in the same boat as you, Pete," answered Jeff. "I studied for Mrs. Russell's history test until 1:00 a.m. last week, but I got my usual 'C.'

"Yeah, I have the same problem. I study, but I don't seem to remember what I study. In psychology class, Mrs. Lloyd said that there's a big difference between studying and learning. She said that studying is the process we use to learn – you know, like you study spelling in order to learn. But to REMEMBER what we study requires us to use both our short-term and long-term memory. I remember her saying, 'To be smart, you must improve your retention ability – that is, your ability to remember.'"

EDCON PUBLISHING

STUDYING AND RETENTION

"Well," said Jeff, "I can tell by my history grade that I could sure use some of that retention ability."

Pete and Jeff see Mrs. Lloyd walking toward them.

"Oh, hi, Mrs. Lloyd," said Jeff. "Pete and I were just talking about Mr. Avery's prize – the ride to the Roller Dance in his antique car. We'd really like to win, but we need help in learning how to raise our test scores.
"I studied until 1:00 a.m. for my last history test, and I received the same grade I always get – a 'C.' I need to know *how* to study."

"And how to learn – and how to remember," said Pete. "We need a game plan."

"We sure do!" agreed Jeff.

"Hold on, boys – one thing at a time. First, it's important for you to know a little more about HOW we learn. For example, psychologists tell us that about 83% of our learning is achieved using our eyes, and about 10% is by hearing. Smell, touch, and taste account for a much smaller percentage of our learning."

"You mean if we ate our history book, we would learn something?" joked Jeff.

STUDYING AND RETENTION

"Yeah," said Pete. "Give me a chapter four sandwich."

"Very funny, boys," laughed Mrs. Lloyd. "I'm sure you would both learn something.

> **SEE & HEAR**
> **50%**

"A recent study indicates that when you combine your learning modes, for example, you SEE and HEAR something at the same time, you increase your chances of remembering it. "So, it's important to know HOW you learn, as well as the best way for you to remember it once you've learned it. If you SEE and HEAR it at the same time, you will have a 50% chance of remembering it.

> **SEE & HEAR & SAY**
> **70%**

"If you SEE & HEAR & SAY it, you'll have a 70% chance of remembering.

> **SEE & HEAR & SAY & DO**
> **90%**

"And if you SEE & HEAR & SAY & DO it, you have a 90% chance of remembering.

"Now, to improve both your short-term and long-term memory, you can use one of the following techniques:

> **MENTAL REHEARSAL**
>
> **TALKING**

"Mental Rehearsal – repeat the information in your mind until you can recall it.

EDCON PUBLISHING

"Talking – speaking out loud as you review the material to be learned. This really helps those students who learn better by hearing.

THE WHY

ORDERING

"The Why – this is really for your internal motivation. Knowing why you have to learn the material is a must. If you don't think it's important to learn, you sure won't learn much.

"Ordering – keep the information to be learned in a sequential or logical order. It might be necessary to rearrange the material.

WRITING

MNEMONIC

"Writing – copying notes from your textbook, or re-copying classroom notes will help you concentrate and reinforce your learning.

"Mnemonic Strategies – organizing information so it's easy to remember. For example, *'30 days hath September...'* Well, that's the start of a poem we learned to help us remember the number of days in each month.

ADDING

RE-CODING

"Adding, or chaining – learning to add parts, groups of letters and numbers together until you've learned all the material.

STUDYING AND RETENTION

"And re-coding – organizing the information that is to be learned into smaller parts or patterns. For example, MT. TOWMAR would help you remember the eight techniques we just used.

"Let's try our short-term memory. Using the first letter as our clue, what would MT. TOWMAR stand for? The **M** would be **MENTAL REHEARSAL**. The **T**, **TALKING**. The second **T** would be **THE WHY**. The **O**, ordering. The **W, WRITING**. The **M, MNEMONIC STRATEGIES**. The **A, ADDING** (or chaining). And the **R**, for **RE-CODING**. Together, they spell MT. TOWMAR.

"By using these techniques and combining your learning modes, you'll improve your learning skills and your attention abilities. This will make you smarter, and give you a good chance to win Mr. Avery's contest."

Jeff smiled. "Thanks for your help, Mrs. Lloyd. If Pete or I win, we'll give you a ride – and maybe buy you a history sandwich! See you later."

*   *   *   *   *

"I don't believe it!" said Nancy to her friend. "I just heard Pete and Jeff talking to Mrs. Lloyd about studying. I believe they're going to try and win Mr. Avery's contest!"

"It's a good thing we decided to review some of our notes from last year's study skills course," replied Alice.

"Yeah," said Nancy. "I remember the first class was really a surprise for us. Mr. Burner explained how important it was for all of us to eat a balanced breakfast. He said that breakfast was the most important meal of the day for us maturing, young adults – and he looked right at me when he said it."

"That's right, he did!" said Alice. "But he also said that we should concentrate in 5 areas:

> **TIME MANAGEMENT**
> **READING**

"1. TIME MANAGEMENT – and this included when and where to study.
2. READING – for understanding and vocabulary.

> **LISTENING**
> **TAKING NOTES**
> **REVIEWING**

3. LISTENING – for improving concentration and memory.
4. TAKING NOTES – both in class and from a textbook.
5. REVIEWING – a continuous process for being prepared.

"Mr. Burner said that to learn study skills, you had to think backwards. By reviewing your notes, you would be reinforcing the information you had learned earlier in the unit.

STUDYING AND RETENTION

"And he often repeated the statement, *'The biggest mistake students make is trying to take too many notes and not being able to pick out the important concepts or ideas.'*
"You can't re-write the book! Learn what's important, and condense it."

"Okay," said Nancy. "Let's start with the first one Mr. Burner gave us – **TIME MANAGEMENT**. Remember, he said everybody had twenty-four hours a day, and some of it could be used to study. But to be meaningful, study time must be

---

**IN TUNE WITH OUR PERSONALITY
PERFORMED IN A QUIET PLACE
ACCOMPLISHED IN SMALL BLOCKS OF TIME."**

"I really believe I learn better in short segments of time," said Kim. "If I try to study for more than 15 or 20 minutes, my mind wanders or I fall asleep."

"I agree," said Nancy. "I like to get up real early in the morning, about 5:00 a.m. It's quiet, and my brothers don't bug me."

"Really," said Kim. "That's what I need. A quiet place to study. I need to read, not only for speed, but for understanding. The two seem to go together. And for learning, you've got to be able to remember what you've read."

EDCON PUBLISHING

Alice addressed her two friends. "I've been reading a complete paragraph, covering it up, and asking myself what I remember. Then I re-read it to see if I've missed anything. Then I take each paragraph and pick out the important terms and concepts and condense them for my notes. This helps me remember, keeps me actively involved in learning, and prepares me for each review session.

"Concentration is an easy one for us athletes. You must apply all your energy, focus all your attention, on the one thing you are doing. Then you will be successful.

"The problem most of us have is we let our mind drift, and don't concentrate on the present task.

"Developing the art of critical listening, or active listening, is another skill we must learn. We must think about what is being said – not allow our mind to wander. And we must be involved with the speaker."

"Note taking must condense information," said Nancy. "Don't write everything! Learn to take down only the important facts. The secret of note taking is selecting the key words or phrases from each paragraph and condensing them to short, understandable statements.

1. **INVOLVED**
2. **CONDENSE**
3. **REVIEW**
4. **REINFORCE**

"Good notes help you to keep INVOLVED in the learning process," continued Nancy. "CONDENSE what is said or written, prepare for the REVIEW, and REINFORCE the material."

STUDYING AND RETENTION

Alice piped up. "I remember Mr. Burner saying that different courses require different study techniques, and even that teachers teaching the same subject require different study techniques."

"Yeah, I remember that," said Kim. "And also, that's when he stressed the importance of reviewing. It helps you prepare you for the pop quizzes, and lets you learn the material, so at test time, you know it cold."

"Well," said Alice, "that was a good review. But, we had better get to our next class."

*   *   *   *   *

After listening to these students, it's easy to see that there's a lot more to studying and retention than we might have thought.

Mr. Avery's prize might have led to self-motivation, but, as the boys learned, they had to conquer MT. TOWMAR:

M - **MENTAL REHEARSAL**
T - **TALKING SKILLS**

T - **THE WAY**
O - **ORDERING**
W - **WRITING**
M - **MNEMONICS**
A - **ADDING**
R - **RE-CODING**

EDCON PUBLISHING

And Nancy, Alice, and Kim knew that they had to improve in the areas of:

NUTRITION
SELF-MOTIVATION
READING TO REMEMBER
LISTENING SKILLS
TIME-MANAGEMENT
NOTE TAKING
REVIEWING

Through the years, the instruments of learning haven't changed much. Internal motivation, coupled with the necessary learning skills, will still carry all students toward successful achievement. It's important for every student to learn and practice the skills of studying and retention.

Promise yourself that you will begin today.

STUDYING AND RETENTION

MATCHING

Match the techniques in Column A to their definitions in Column B.

COLUMN A	COLUMN B
_____ 1. studying	A. internal motivation
_____ 2. talking	B. "Thirty Days hath September"
_____ 3. self-motivation	C. realistic and obtainable
_____ 4. writing	D. organizing into smaller parts
_____ 5. goal	E. 50% chance of remembering
_____ 6. mnemonic	F. help keep you involved in the learning process
_____ 7. see and hear	G. repeating information in your mind until you can recall it
_____ 8. ordering	H. 70% chance of remembering
_____ 9. see, hear & say	I. grouping or adding letters together
_____ 10. see, hear, say, & do	J. helps those who learn by hearing
_____ 11. re-coding	K. copying notes for reinforcement
_____ 12. mental rehearsal	L. a MUST for learning
_____ 13. chaining	M. 90% chance of remembering
_____ 14. The Why	N. process used for learning
_____ 15. Good notes	O. keeping information in logical or sequential order

Answers can be found on page 46.

EDCON PUBLISHING

FILL-IN

Add the correct word to the sentences below.

A. Reinforce   C. involved

B. review   D. Condense

Good notes help you to:

1. Keep _____ in the learning process.

2. _____ what is said or written.

3. Prepare for the _____.

4. _____ the material to be learned.

Answers can be found on page 46.

STUDYING AND RETENTION

FILL-IN

Explain how the following words or terms relate to studying, learning, and/or retention. Use one or two sentences.

1. Time management _____

    _____

    _____

2. Nutrition _____

    _____

    _____

3. Reading to remember _____

    _____

    _____

4. Listening skills _____

    _____

    _____

5. Note taking _____

    _____

    _____

6. _____

    _____

EDCON PUBLISHING

ANSWER KEY

LEARNING HOW TO TAKE A TEST

SENTENCE COMPLETION

1. study
2. mental attitude
3. responsibility
4. afraid
5. meal
6. early and ready
7. desk tops
8. Listen

9. directions, questions
10. format
11. eyes
12. Concentrate
13. grammar
14. guess
15. rush

TEST WISENESS

SENTENCE COMPLETION

1. D
2. G
3. C
4. B
5. F
6. E
7. H
8. A
9. J
10. I

ANSWER KEY

STUDYING AND RETENTION

MATCHING

1. N
2. J
3. L
4. K
5. C
6. B
7. E
8. O
9. H
10. M
11. D
12. G
13. I
14. A
15. F

FILL IN

1. C
2. D
3. B
4. A

EDCON PUBLISHING

Notes

Notes

EDCON PUBLISHING